I Like the RAIN

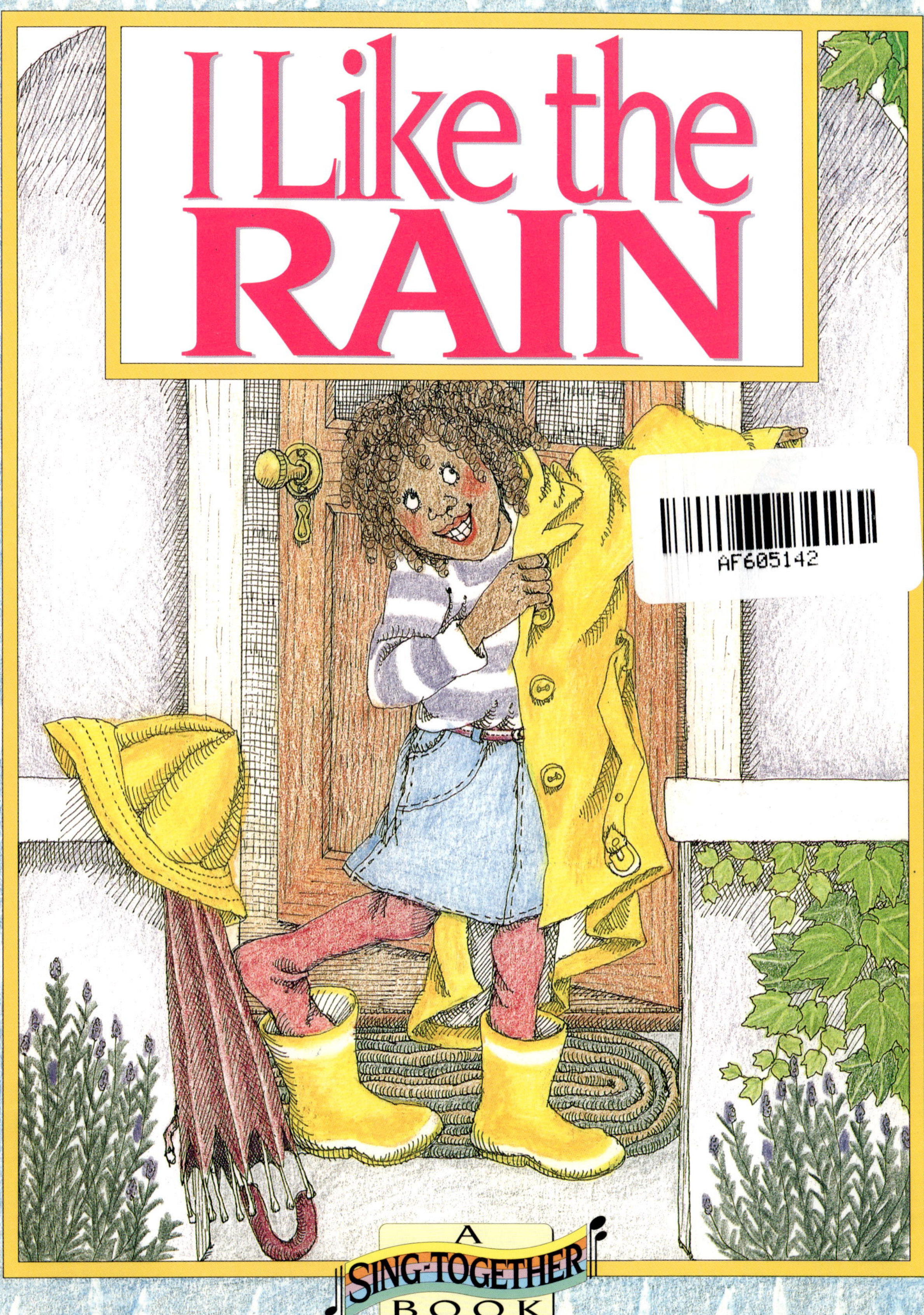

A SING-TOGETHER BOOK

I like the rain.
I like the rain.
R-a-i-n.
I like the rain.

I like the snow.
I like the snow.
S-n-o-w.
I like the snow.

I like the wind.
I like the wind.
W-i-n-d.
I like the wind.

I like the heat.
I like the heat.
H-e-a-t.
I like the heat.

I like the hail.
I like the hail.
H-a-i-l.
I like the hail.

I cheer for the weather.
Hip, hip, hooray!
'Cause I like the outdoors,
And I like to play.

Hip, hip,
hooray!

I like to play.
I like to play.
P-l-a-y.

I like to play.